·A RANDOM HOUSE TELL ME ABOUT BOOK·

EVERYDAY THINGS
& HOW THEY WORK

By Steve Parker

Illustrated by Peter Bull
& Ian Moores

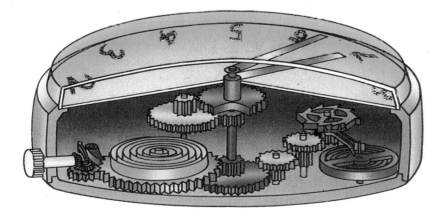

RANDOM HOUSE  NEW YORK

Contents

First American edition, 1991

Library of Congress Cataloging-in-Publication Data
Parker, Steve.
Everyday things & how they work / by Steve Parker; illustrated by Peter Bull and Ian Moores.
p. cm.—(A Random House tell me about book)
Includes index.
Summary: Ordinary appliances and gadgets around the house get a new look, with a view to understanding their origin, purpose, and function. Readers learn how to think up ideas for new and special tools and appliances.
ISBN 0–679–80866–3
1. Household appliances—Juvenile literature.
[1. Household appliances—Miscellanea.
2. Questions and answers.]
I. Bull, Peter, ill. II. Moores, Ian, ill.
III. Title IV. Title: Everyday things and how they work.
V. Series.
TX298.P38 1991b
643'.6—dc20
91–213

Manufactured in Spain 1 2 3 4 5 6 7 8 9 10

Where does electricity come from?

The electricity in a house comes from a power plant. In all power plants, some kind of power pushes a huge wheel around very fast. This wheel turns an enormous machine called a generator. It is the generator that makes the electricity. Some power plants get power from burning coal or oil. Others make electricity from the power of running water or from nuclear power.

ELECTRICITY WARNING

The electricity in wall sockets is very powerful. Never poke things into the holes in a socket. It could kill you.

Most power plants have more than one generator so they can produce lots of electricity.

A transformer increases the strength of the electricity so it can be carried by wires for long distances.

ELECTRICITY FACTS

• Electricity travels as fast as light—186,000 miles per second! It could go around the earth 15 times a second.

• The strength of electricity is measured in volts. In most homes in the U.S.A. it is 110 or 220 volts. The big wires from a power plant carry more than 500,000 volts.

Towers called pylons hold the wires far away from the ground so that people below are safe.

MAKE STATIC ELECTRICITY

Static electricity is electricity which stays still. To make a small amount of static electricity, rub a balloon on a woolen sweater. See how it makes the balloon stick to a wall.

The electricity comes into each house through a meter. Dials show how much electricity has been used.

At a substation another transformer makes the electricity less strong so that it is ready to be used in houses.

The electricity flows from the substation to the houses through underground cables or overhead wires.

How do light bulbs shine?

Light bulbs shine because the very thin wire inside, the filament, gets extremely hot. When you turn on a switch, the electricity flows along a wire and into the light bulb. The electricity has to force its way through the filament, making it so hot that it glows, giving out light.

Ask an adult to help you.

To make a circuit, electricity has to flow in a circle.

1 Attach two pieces of wire to a small block of wood with two thumbtacks.

2 Join the end of one wire to a battery and the end of the other wire to a bulb and battery.

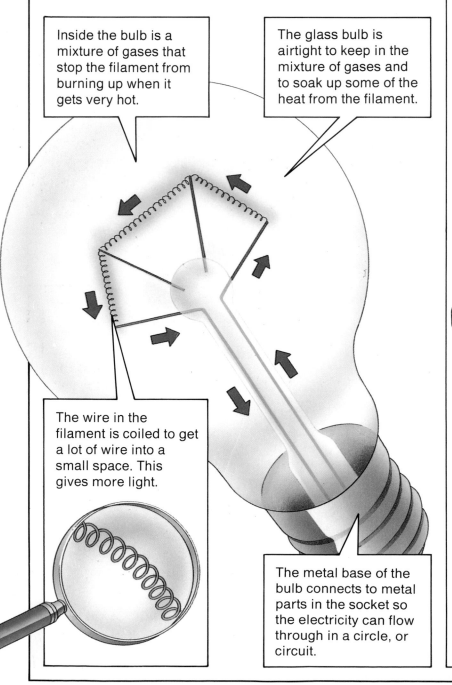

Inside the bulb is a mixture of gases that stop the filament from burning up when it gets very hot.

The glass bulb is airtight to keep in the mixture of gases and to soak up some of the heat from the filament.

The wire in the filament is coiled to get a lot of wire into a small space. This gives more light.

The metal base of the bulb connects to metal parts in the socket so the electricity can flow through in a circle, or circuit.

3 Hook one end of a paper clip under one of the thumbtacks.

4 When the paper clip touches both tacks it makes a circuit and switches the bulb on. Switch the bulb off by moving the paper clip away from one tack.

Why do some lights flicker?

Some lights flicker when they are first switched on because the special gas inside them is too cold for the electric current to flow through it properly. When the gas heats up, the light becomes a steady glow. These are called fluorescent lights.

The inside of the tube is coated with a chemical that glows when it is hit by the particles—this gives us light.

The gas inside the tube gives off tiny invisible particles as the electric current flows through it.

How does a flashlight work?

A flashlight has batteries inside it. Batteries supply the electricity to light the bulb. When a flashlight is switched on, a circuit is made between the batteries and the bulb.

The switch slides along to make contact and complete the circuit, or pushes back to break the circuit and turn off the bulb.

OFF

ON

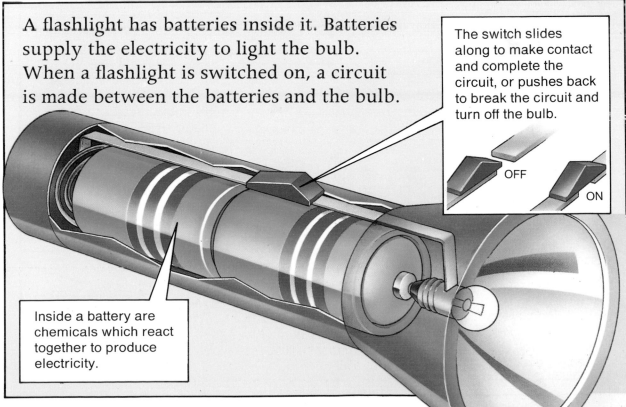

Inside a battery are chemicals which react together to produce electricity.

How do stoves work?

An electric stove turns electricity into heat. The electricity pushes its way through a special wire called an element, which becomes very hot. Each element is held inside a metal ring either on top of or inside the oven. As the element heats up, the heat passes through the ring to cook the food.

COOKING FACTS

● Some new stoves "cook with light." Instead of an element, they have a powerful lamp that shines light and heat up from below. This is the same type of lamp as in a strong car headlight!

● The first cookbook, *Hedypathia*, was written by an ancient Greek named Archestratus 2,400 years ago.

Inside each ring there is a special powder which lets the heat through to the ring but stops the electric current.

Powder

Element

A control knob changes the amount of electricity going to each element, to make it warmer or cooler.

Some rings have a thermostat, a switch which turns off when too hot and on when too cool. As the switch heats up, it bends away to break the circuit. As it cools it straightens and makes the circuit again.

Too hot, switch off

Too cool, switch on

The oven door and sides contain an insulating material which stops most of the heat from escaping from the oven.

An electric fan blows the hot air around the oven. This helps to spread the heat so that the food cooks evenly.

How do microwave ovens work?

Microwaves are invisible waves, like radio waves and X-ray waves. When they are beamed strongly into food, they make the watery parts vibrate, or shake, and become hot. This heat is passed through the food and cooks it from the inside out.

The magnetron is the part of a microwave oven that makes the microwaves.

The microwaves are beamed at a metal fan which scatters them around the oven.

Beams of microwaves

Even with a fan, some parts of the food may become hotter than others. So a turntable rotates the food for even cooking.

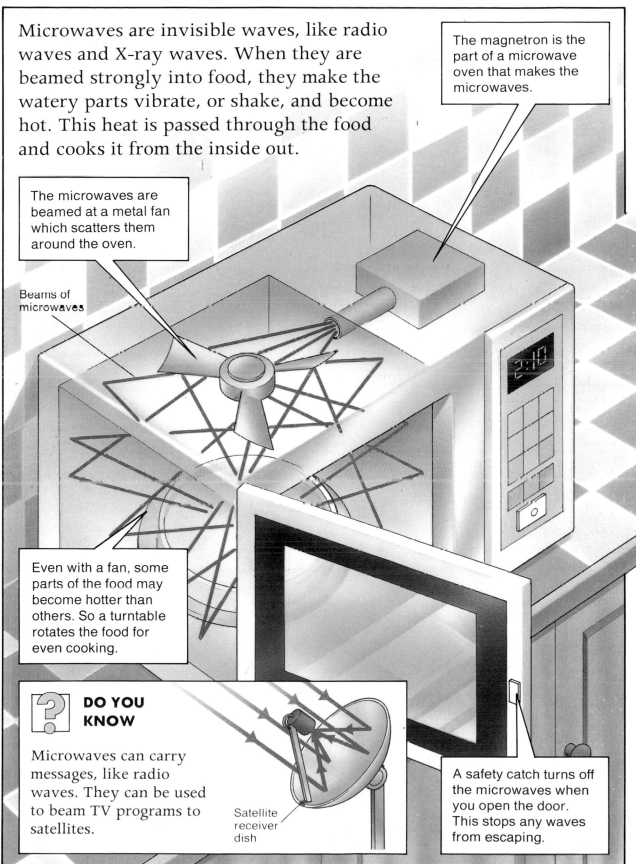

? DO YOU KNOW

Microwaves can carry messages, like radio waves. They can be used to beam TV programs to satellites.

Satellite receiver dish

A safety catch turns off the microwaves when you open the door. This stops any waves from escaping.

How does a vacuum bottle work?

A vacuum bottle keeps drinks hot by stopping the movement of heat out of the bottle. There is a gap between the bottle's outer case and the inner container. This gap has nothing in it, not even air—it is a vacuum. Heat cannot move very easily across a vacuum, so it is not lost through the sides of the flask. And a tight-fitting stopper prevents heat from leaking out of the top of the flask.

VACUUM FACTS

● The first vacuum bottle was invented by Scottish scientist James Dewar in 1892. The bottle was used to keep oxygen in liquid form at very cold temperatures, well below zero!

● Space is almost a vacuum, but there are some things floating in it, mostly specks of dust and particles of gas.

The stopper is made of thick plastic or cork. These materials are good insulators and so they keep heat in.

Air in the gap would carry heat from the container to the case to be lost. The vacuum prevents this.

The walls of the container are shiny. They reflect the heat waves from the liquid.

As well as keeping heat in, bottles keep heat out. They keep things cold too.

DO YOU KNOW

In 1973, a panel on the Skylab space station came off in space. The astronauts got too hot in the sun's glare. So they fixed up a shiny shield to reflect the heat, like the lining in a vacuum bottle.

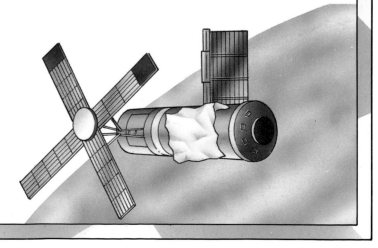

How do refrigerators keep food cold?

A refrigerator keeps food cold by moving heat from inside to outside. A liquid flows around a circuit of pipes. As it flows it changes from a liquid to a gas and takes up heat from inside the refrigerator. The pipes carry the gas outside and give off heat.

? DO YOU KNOW

In very cold countries refrigerators are used to keep the food from getting *too* cold.

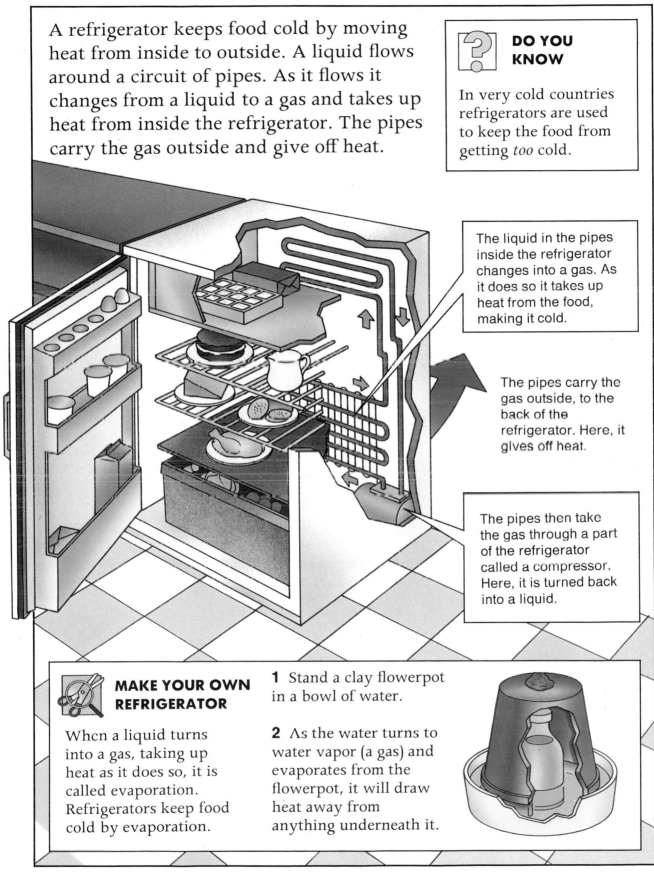

The liquid in the pipes inside the refrigerator changes into a gas. As it does so it takes up heat from the food, making it cold.

The pipes carry the gas outside, to the back of the refrigerator. Here, it gives off heat.

The pipes then take the gas through a part of the refrigerator called a compressor. Here, it is turned back into a liquid.

MAKE YOUR OWN REFRIGERATOR

When a liquid turns into a gas, taking up heat as it does so, it is called evaporation. Refrigerators keep food cold by evaporation.

1 Stand a clay flowerpot in a bowl of water.

2 As the water turns to water vapor (a gas) and evaporates from the flowerpot, it will draw heat away from anything underneath it.

How do vacuum cleaners work?

Inside a vacuum cleaner there is an electric motor which drives a fan around very fast. As the fan whirls around it sucks air in through a nozzle and hose attached to the cleaner. Dust and dirt are sucked in with the air.

As the fan whirls around it pushes air out at one end. At the same time it pulls more air in through the hose.

The air flows through a paper bag in the cleaner. Dust and dirt cannot pass through the bag. They are trapped.

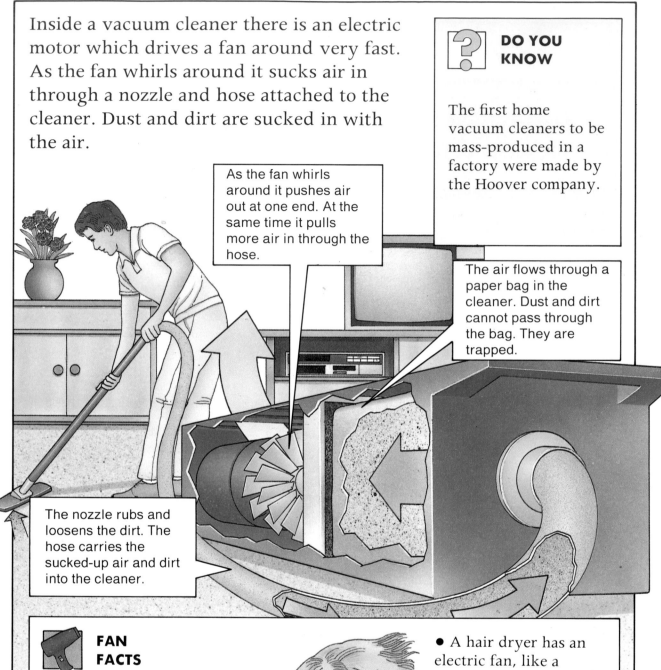

The nozzle rubs and loosens the dirt. The hose carries the sucked-up air and dirt into the cleaner.

FAN FACTS

• A car also has an electric fan. The fan draws cool air past the engine and radiator to stop the engine from overheating—particularly when the car is standing still.

• A hair dryer has an electric fan, like a vacuum cleaner. But it works in the opposite way. It sucks air in at the back of the dryer and blows it out through the nozzle at the front. A heater element inside warms the air as it passes through.

How does a washing machine wash?

A washing machine has a drum inside it that turns around and around, mixing dirty clothes up with soap and water. The soap and water loosen dirt and stains from the material, and then clean water rinses away the soap and the dirt. Finally, the drum spins around very fast to fling off water and to partly dry the load.

? DO YOU KNOW

Soap works by getting between the greasy dirt and the cloth. Each particle of soap has one "grease-loving" end and one "water-loving" end.

In soapy water, a piece of dirt is soon surrounded by a layer of soap particles, with their grease-loving ends stuck to the dirt and their water-loving ends pulling toward the water. The particles loosen the dirt, which lifts off the cloth and floats away.

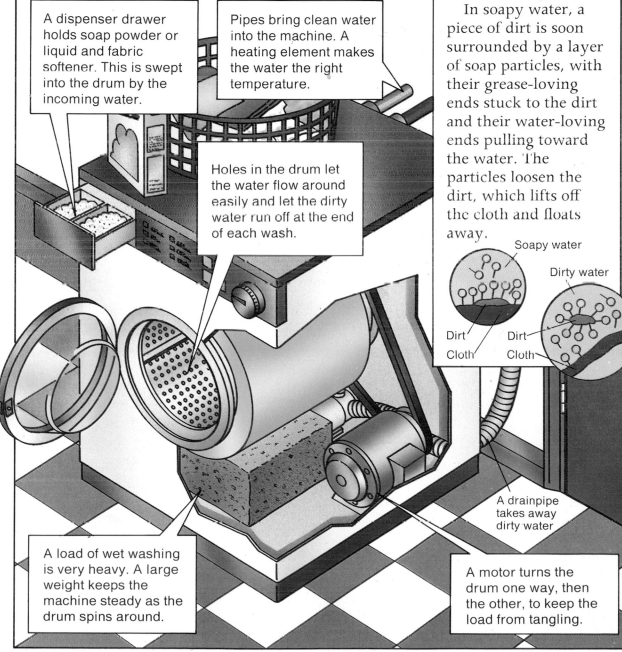

A dispenser drawer holds soap powder or liquid and fabric softener. This is swept into the drum by the incoming water.

Pipes bring clean water into the machine. A heating element makes the water the right temperature.

Holes in the drum let the water flow around easily and let the dirty water run off at the end of each wash.

Soapy water

Dirty water

Dirt

Dirt

Cloth

Cloth

A load of wet washing is very heavy. A large weight keeps the machine steady as the drum spins around.

A drainpipe takes away dirty water

A motor turns the drum one way, then the other, to keep the load from tangling.

What is a telecommunications network?

Telephone, television, and radio all form a telecommunications network which sends and receives messages over a long distance. Telephone calls are turned into electrical signals which are then sent along telephone wires. The signals for television and radio are sent along wires to a transmitter where they are changed into radio waves, one of the many kinds of invisible waves which pass through the air around us all the time.

The transmitter gets electrical signals from the station and sends them out as radio waves.

A telephone receives electrical signals along a wire and turns these signals back into sound.

An antenna picks up radio waves passing through the air, and the radio turns them into sound.

MESSAGE FACTS

● The earliest ways of sending messages used flags, fires, smoke, lamps, or drums. Only very simple messages could be sent.

● Today we can send television pictures from the U.S.A. to Europe and back via space satellite, 30 times in one second!

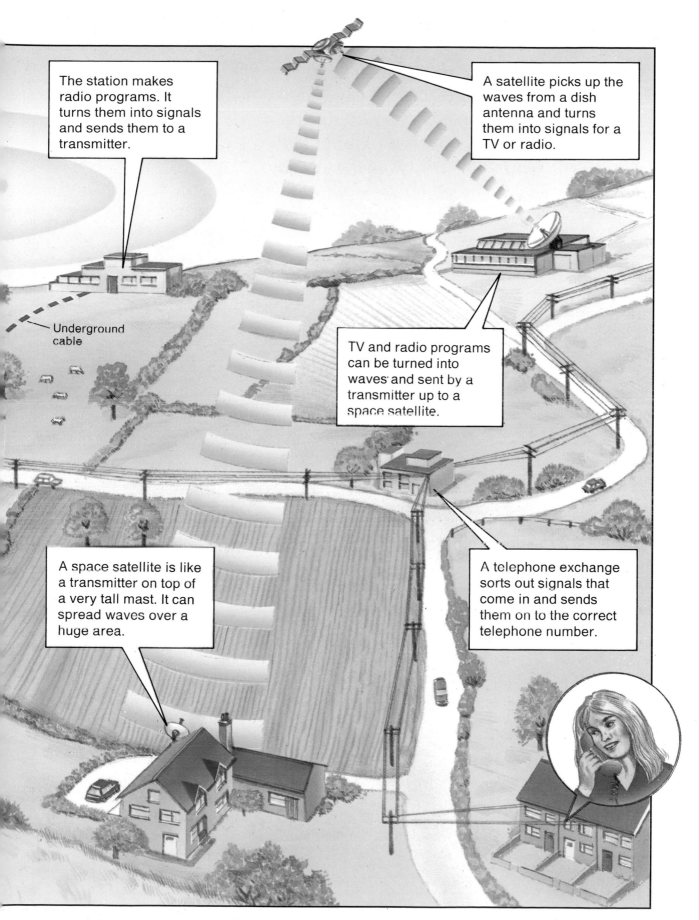

The station makes radio programs. It turns them into signals and sends them to a transmitter.

A satellite picks up the waves from a dish antenna and turns them into signals for a TV or radio.

Underground cable

TV and radio programs can be turned into waves and sent by a transmitter up to a space satellite.

A space satellite is like a transmitter on top of a very tall mast. It can spread waves over a huge area.

A telephone exchange sorts out signals that come in and sends them on to the correct telephone number.

15

How do radios work?

A radio picks up, or detects, radio waves with its antenna and turns the waves into tiny electrical signals with its tuner. It then makes the signals stronger in its amplifier and turns them into sound waves with its speakers. Radios run on electrical power, either from batteries inside the case or from a plug and socket.

A volume knob alters the power of the amplifier, which controls the loudness of the sound waves.

A tuning knob selects which station's waves the radio receives. This is shown on a tuning dial.

Antenna

The amplifier boosts the weak signals it receives from the tuner, so that they are strong enough to work the speakers.

Speaker

Electrical signals at the back of the speaker make its front part shake, or vibrate, producing sounds.

 RADIO FACTS

• The golden age of radio was from about 1925 to 1955. After this, television took over.

• The first radio broadcast was to ships in the Atlantic Ocean by an American professor, Reginald Fessenden, in 1906.

• The first radio station to broadcast regular programs was KDKA in Pittsburgh, Pennsylvania. It began sending out music and sports programs in 1920.

How do telephones work?

A telephone changes the sound of your voice into electrical signals and sends them along wires to the telephone exchange. From here, the signals are sent to the telephone of the person you are talking to, where they are changed back into sounds. Signals also travel from the other person's telephone to yours.

A switch in the telephone turns it off when you put the receiver down. Or you can press the switch if you want to make another call.

A small loudspeaker in the receiver's earpiece turns signals into sound waves, which you can hear.

A loudspeaker in the base makes a chirping or ringing noise, which means that someone is telephoning you.

A microphone in the mouthpiece turns your voice's sound waves into electrical signals, which travel along the wire into the base.

MAKE A TELEPHONE

1 Find two clean, empty yogurt pots and make a small hole in the base of each one.

2 Thread the end of a long piece of string through each hole, and tie it in a knot. With a friend, pull the pots apart so that the string stretches fairly tight.

3 Speak into your pot while your friend holds the other pot to his or her ear. Your pot turns your voice's sound waves into vibrations. These travel along the string and are turned back into sound by the other pot.

How do televisions work?

A television set changes electrical signals into pictures on the screen and sounds from the loudspeaker. The television antenna detects waves sent from the TV transmitter. These waves are turned into signals by the television's tuner. The signals are made more powerful by electronic circuits. Then they are turned into streams of invisible particles called electrons, which are fired by electron guns onto the back of the screen. Where the electrons hit the screen, they make it glow and give off light, forming a picture.

DO YOU KNOW

A survey snowed that, on average, American children watch television for 7 hours each day. So by the time they are 18 years old, they have spent about 4 years watching television— and about 6 years being asleep!

On the inside of the screen are hundreds of tiny dots, in three colors. These glow when hit by electrons.

A shadow mask behind the screen makes sure the electrons from each gun hit the correct color of dots.

The streams of electrons sweep across the screen to build up the image. A picture is produced 30 times a second.

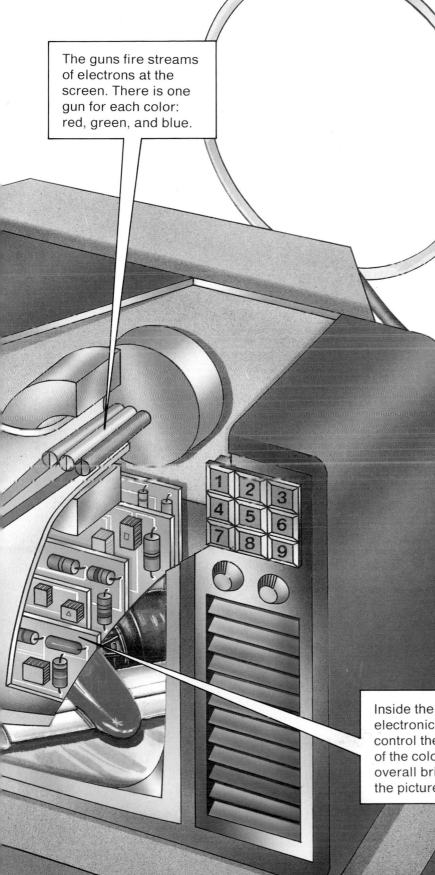

The guns fire streams of electrons at the screen. There is one gun for each color: red, green, and blue.

Inside the set, electronic circuits control the brightness of the colors and the overall brightness of the picture.

MAKE A FLIP BOOK

A television program is actually made up of thousands of still pictures. These flash so quickly before your eyes they appear to be one continuous picture with moving images. You can see how this works by making a flip book.

1 Take an old book and draw a matchstick figure on the corner of one page.

2 Draw the figure in the corner of several pages, changing part of the figure each time. When you flip the pages quickly, the many still pictures blur into a "moving" picture.

How do cassette players work?

Cassette players work by moving a tape past a tape head. A cassette tape contains tiny patches of magnetism, which are codes for the sounds recorded on it. The tape head changes these magnetic codes into electrical signals. The signals are made more powerful by an amplifier and then sent to a loudspeaker, which turns the signals into sounds.

RUB OUT A TAPE

Hold a strong magnet against an old, unwanted tape. It will disturb the magnetic codes and erase most of the recording.

Pattern after erasing

Old recording pattern

The tape head is a small coil of wire on a metal core. As the tape goes past, the magnetic codes create electrical signals in the wire.

Tape

Coil of wire

Core

Most cassette players have a small microphone that allows you to make your own recordings.

A wheel presses the tape against a spinning rod. This pulls the tape past the tape head at a regular speed.

Wheel

Rod

Tape

How do video recorders work?

Like the cassette player, a videocassette recorder (VCR) uses a tape head to read or record magnetic codes on a tape. But these codes contain pictures as well as sounds.

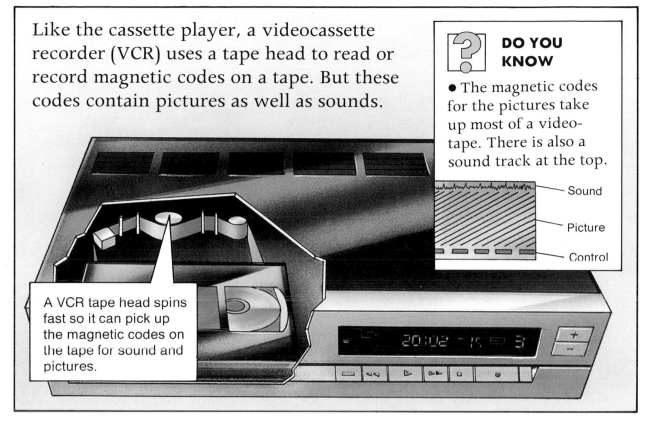

Sound

Picture

Control

A VCR tape head spins fast so it can pick up the magnetic codes on the tape for sound and pictures.

How do calculators work?

A calculator is a simple type of computer. It treats numbers as a series of electrical signals which it can add or subtract using the tiny electrical circuits in a microchip.

The microchip can carry out hundreds of sums each second. It is powered by a small battery.

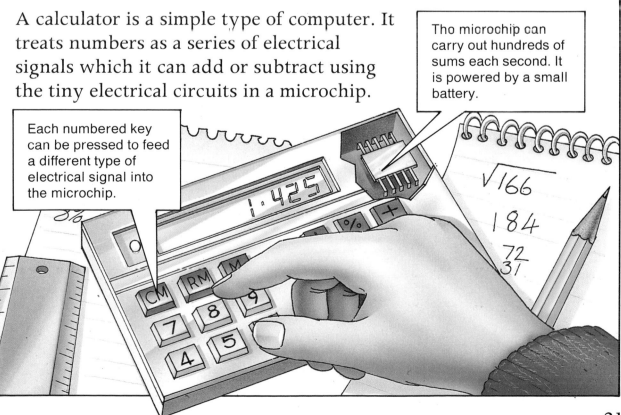

Each numbered key can be pressed to feed a different type of electrical signal into the microchip.

What do computers do?

A computer turns all sorts of information into electrical signals. Information can be fed into and out of a computer using machines called input and output units. A computer can do many different things with this information by following a list of instructions. This list is called a program, and it is stored inside the computer.

? DO YOU KNOW

Computers are used to do everything from playing chess to flying aircraft, forecasting the weather, and storing fingerprints for the police.

COMPUTER FACTS

● The heart of a computer is a Central Processing Unit (CPU). This is where the electrical signals from an input unit are altered according to the program instructions and sent to the output unit.

● A computer has its own memory. Any information in this memory is lost when the computer is switched off, so information is stored on disks or tapes.

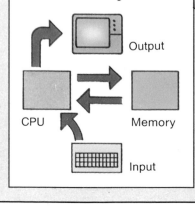

CPU

Memory

Output

Input

1 The major input unit is a typewriter keyboard. Information is typed into the computer and shown on a screen.

Keyboard

CPU

TV screen

Joystick

Mouse

2 Other input units include a joystick and a mouse. These can move information around on the screen.

22

Printer

4 The major output unit is a television screen. Information can also be put onto paper by a printer.

Disk

Tape

3 Information can be sent from the computer and stored as magnetic codes on disks or tapes for later use.

COMPUTER HISTORY

● The first electronic computer was ENIAC, made in 1946 at the University of Pennsylvania. It took up the floor space of an average house, but was only as powerful as a modern pocket computer.

● One of the most powerful computers in the world is the CYBER Model 205-444 system, which can do 800 million sums a second.

23

How does a camera take pictures?

To take a picture, a camera lets in light from a scene or an image in front of it and directs the light onto a piece of photographic film. The light affects the chemicals that coat the film and make a picture on it. When the film is developed, it is bathed in chemicals which make this picture permanent. The picture can then be printed onto photographic paper.

A shutter button opens the shutter for a fraction of a second to let the right amount of light into the camera.

 MAKE A CAMERA

This simple pinhole camera shows how a real camera works.

1 With an adult's help, cut one side out of an empty cardboard box. Paint the inside black.

2 Tape a piece of thin tracing paper over the missing side.

3 Make a tiny pinhole in the middle of the side opposite.

4 Set up the camera in a room with the pinhole side facing a bright window. Put an object in front of the window and cover up any other sources of light.

5 The pinhole is the lens. It directs the light onto the tracing paper, which is the film. You should see an upside-down picture of the window on the film. A real camera lens also turns the picture upside down.

Tracing paper

Pinhole

Picture

Box

Photographic film is a long roll of plastic with a chemical coating. It winds along for each new photograph.

24

When you look through the viewfinder, you see the same scene or image that the camera will photograph.

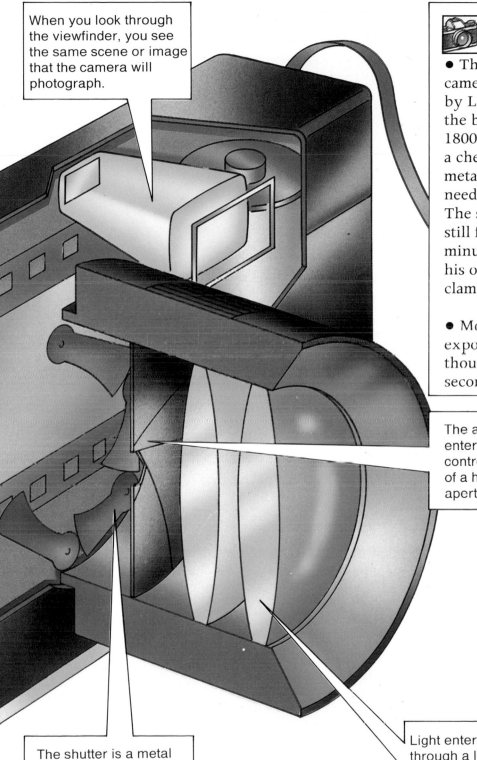

 CAMERA FACTS

• The first practical camera was invented by Louis Daguerre at the beginning of the 1800s. Its "film" was a chemically treated metal plate, which needed a lot of light. The subject had to sit still for up to ten minutes, often with his or her head in a clamp to keep it still.

• Modern films allow exposure times of one thousandth of a second.

The amount of light entering the camera is controlled by the size of a hole—the aperture.

The shutter is a metal flap which is usually closed. It opens briefly to let light pass through onto the film.

Light enters the camera through a lens. This is a curved piece of glass that focuses the light to make the picture sharp and clear.

Why do some doors open by themselves?

A door that opens automatically, or by itself, does so because an electronic sensor tells it when someone is nearby. The sensor can be a light beam or a pressure mat.

A light beam shines from a sender to a receiver. If the beam is blocked, the receiver tells the doors to open.

A pressure mat contains a switch. When a person stands on it, the weight closes the switch and makes the doors open.

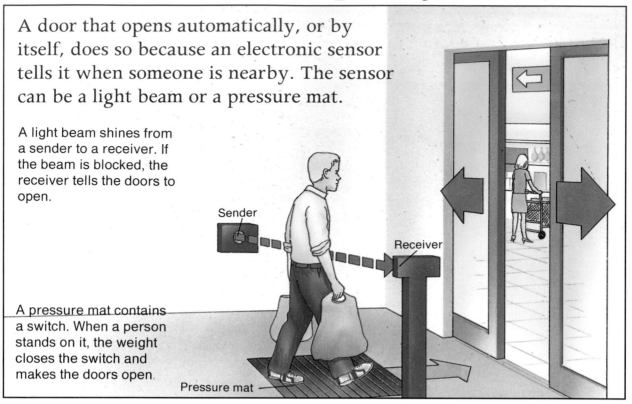

Sender

Receiver

Pressure mat

What are bar codes?

A bar code contains information in the form of black bars of different thicknesses. A machine called an optical scanner can turn this code into electronic signals.

A bar code contains information about the object it is printed on, like its price and identification number.

The scanner sends the information to a computerized cash register, which shows it on the display.

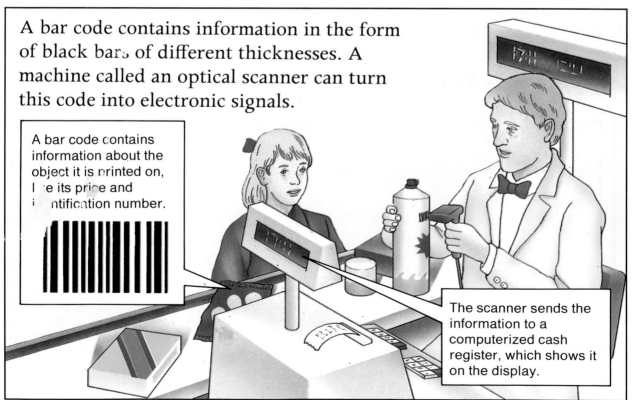

How do locks work?

To lock a door, a bolt moves out of the lock and slides into the door frame. Unlocking the door slides this bolt back. The key turns a cylinder which makes the bolt move.

When the door is locked, small springs push a row of pins into the metal cylinder so it cannot be turned.

The notches on the key push the pins free of the cylinder so the key can turn the cylinder and move the bolt.

DO YOU KNOW

The Yale lock was invented in 1865, but it works in the same way as the locks used in ancient Egypt.

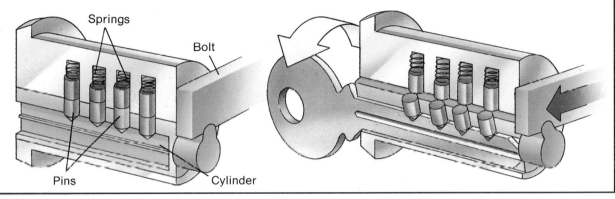

Springs

Bolt

Pins

Cylinder

How do doorbells work?

A doorbell uses electricity to make a hammer strike a bell. When you press the bell button, a magnet is turned on and this pulls the metal hammer against the bell.

The bell button is part of a circuit. Pressing it allows electricity to flow around the circuit to the magnet.

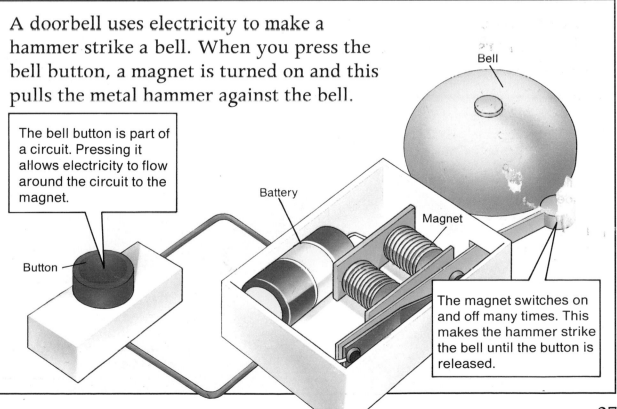

Bell

Button

Battery

Magnet

The magnet switches on and off many times. This makes the hammer strike the bell until the button is released.

How do clocks work?

Inside a clock, a wound-up spring slowly unwinds and turns a notched wheel. This wheel drives a series of other wheels that makes the clock hands move around.

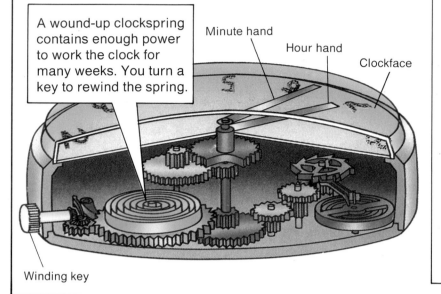

A wound-up clockspring contains enough power to work the clock for many weeks. You turn a key to rewind the spring.

Minute hand

Hour hand

Clockface

Winding key

WATCH FACTS

A digital watch has no springs or wheels. It is powered by a small battery that makes a tiny crystal vibrate, or shake. This produces a stream of electrical signals. A microchip counts the signals and shows the time as a series of changing numbers.

How do scales work?

When something is put into a scale's pan, it presses down on a long bar. This pressure pulls down a spring which makes a pointer move around the scale's numbered face.

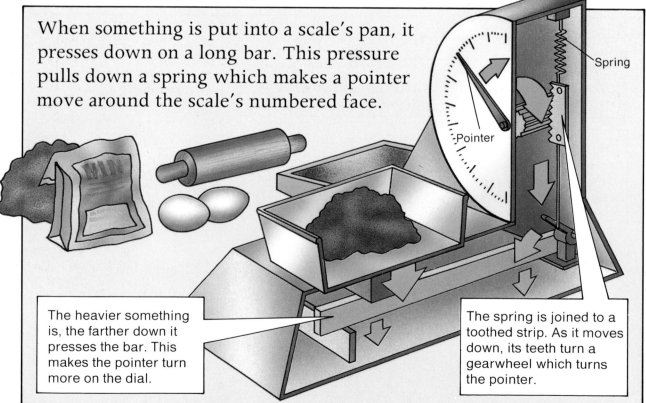

Spring

Pointer

The heavier something is, the farther down it presses the bar. This makes the pointer turn more on the dial.

The spring is joined to a toothed strip. As it moves down, its teeth turn a gearwheel which turns the pointer.

How do screwdrivers work?

A screwdriver is a kind of lever which goes in a circle. A person turns the handle and the force of the turn travels down the shaft to the blade and then to the screw.

At the top of the screwdriver the hand moves through a large circle in order to turn the screwdriver.

At the bottom of the screwdriver the distance to turn is smaller, so greater force is needed here to turn the screw.

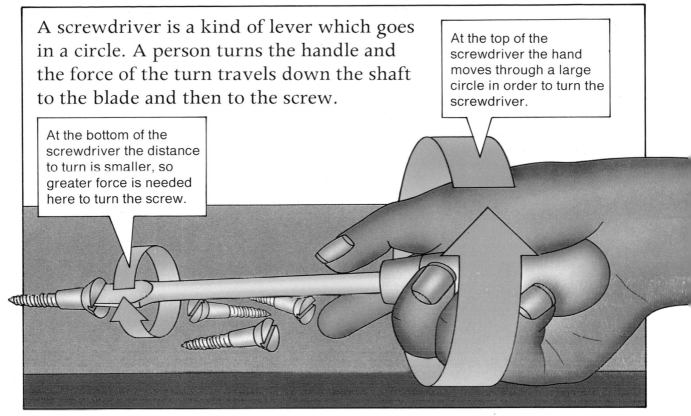

How do can openers work?

A can opener is a kind of double lever. A person squeezes the handles a long way with a small force. This moves the blade a short distance but with great force.

The handles must be kept squeezed together, or the force on the blade will weaken and the lid will push it out.

Turnkey

Once the wedge-shaped blade is pushed into the can, a turnkey must be turned to move the blade along.

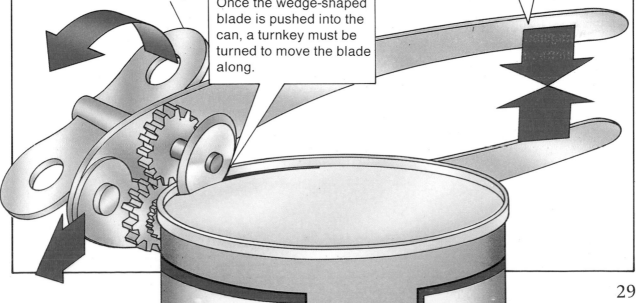

29

How do zippers work?

As a zipper is pulled up, the sliding part presses together two rows of tiny teeth and makes them lock together. To undo a zipper, the slide forces the teeth apart.

In the center of the slide there is a wedge. This separates the two rows of teeth when the slide is pulled down.

There is a small space under each tooth. As the teeth are forced together, each one slides into the space under the tooth above.

How do bicycle gears work?

Bicycle gears control the number of times the back wheel is turned around for each turn of the pedals. The chain is moved to a different-sized cogwheel for each gear.

High gears are for going downhill. You pedal more slowly to produce a fast turn of the back wheel.

Low gears are for going uphill. You pedal faster to produce a slow, strong turn of the back wheel.

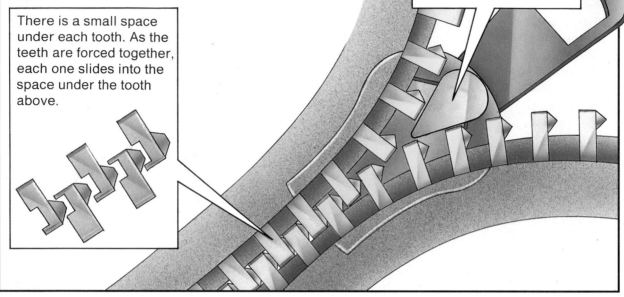

How do bicycle pumps work?

A bicycle pump pulls in air and pushes it through a connecting tube into a bicycle tire. A valve inside the pump controls the flow of air.

When you push the pump handle down, the valve closes, forcing the air inside into the tire.

When you pull the handle out, the valve opens. Air is sucked into the pump, ready for the next push of the handle.

How do aerosol sprays work?

Inside an aerosol can a gas is packed so tightly that it forces the liquid up a tube. When the button is pressed, a hole in the nozzle opens and the contents spray out.

A valve in the nozzle opens to let the gas and liquid out. The small hole changes the liquid into a fine spray.

A gas at high pressure pushes down on the liquid. The can is specially made to withstand the high pressure inside.

Gas

Liquid

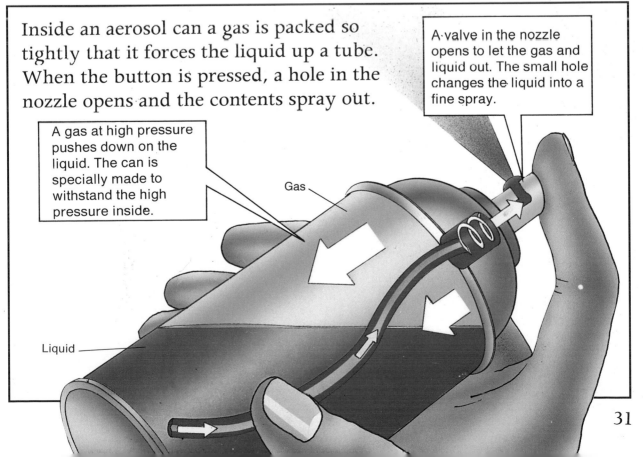

How do car engines work?

Car engines burn gasoline to create the power that makes the car move. When a car is driven, hundreds of small explosions happen in the engine every minute as the gasoline is burned. The explosions happen inside cylinders. In each cylinder, the force of each explosion pushes down a piston. The pistons are connected to a crankshaft. Their movement turns the crankshaft around and this power is carried to the car's transmission.

DO YOU KNOW

Engine power is usually measured in horsepower. This was originally the pulling power of a good farm horse!

An average family car produces about 50–80 horsepower. A Grand Prix racing car produces more than 500 horsepower.

The drive shaft carries the turning power from the transmission and passes it on to the rear wheels.

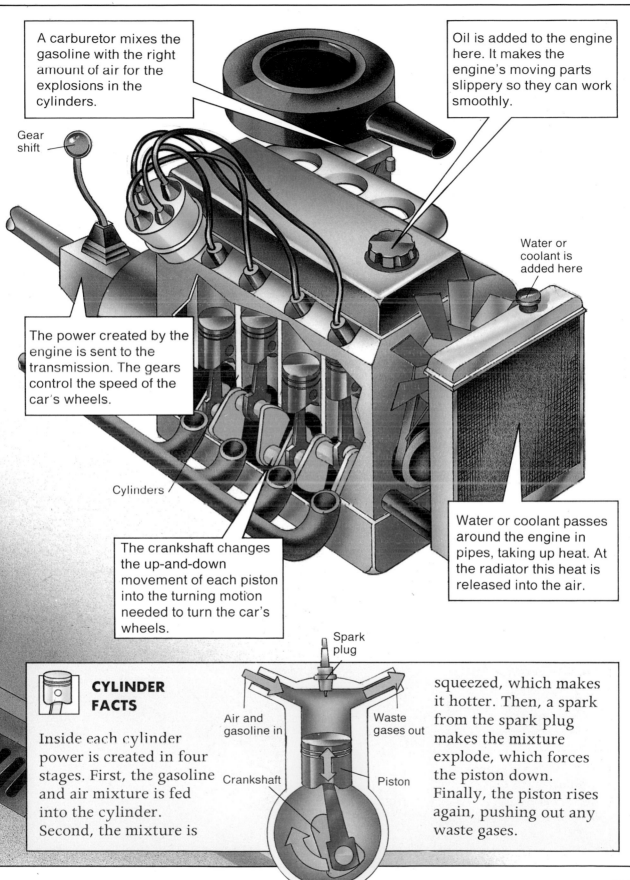

A carburetor mixes the gasoline with the right amount of air for the explosions in the cylinders.

Oil is added to the engine here. It makes the engine's moving parts slippery so they can work smoothly.

Gear shift

Water or coolant is added here

The power created by the engine is sent to the transmission. The gears control the speed of the car's wheels.

Cylinders

The crankshaft changes the up-and-down movement of each piston into the turning motion needed to turn the car's wheels.

Water or coolant passes around the engine in pipes, taking up heat. At the radiator this heat is released into the air.

Spark plug

CYLINDER FACTS

Inside each cylinder power is created in four stages. First, the gasoline and air mixture is fed into the cylinder. Second, the mixture is

Air and gasoline in

Waste gases out

Crankshaft

Piston

squeezed, which makes it hotter. Then, a spark from the spark plug makes the mixture explode, which forces the piston down. Finally, the piston rises again, pushing out any waste gases.

Where does our water come from?

Our water comes from rain that falls into a storage reservoir or trickles through the soil into a river. It is then drawn off in pipes and treated to make it clean and safe to drink. It is pumped to each house along a large pipe under the ground, called a water main. In some houses, water from the main flows up into a cold-water tank in the attic. Usually, the kitchen cold tap is connected directly to the main.

DO YOU KNOW

In countries such as the U.S.A., each person uses up to 80 gallons of water a day. This includes water for drinking and cooking, water for the bath (20 gallons) water for washing clothes, and water for flushing the toilet (5 gallons). In some countries, each person uses about 6 gallons of water a day.

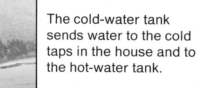

The cold-water tank sends water to the cold taps in the house and to the hot-water tank.

The water main carries water at high pressure from a larger main, usually buried under a nearby road or path.

Hot-water tank

A reservoir is an artificial lake that collects and stores huge amounts of rain and river water.

A pumping station contains huge machines that whirl around, pumping the water up into a water tower.

A water tower stores water high up. This gives it plenty of force to flow down into the water main.

A water treatment plant filters and cleans the water to remove poisonous chemicals and dangerous germs.

HOW TO FILTER WATER

Water treatment plants use large beds of sand, gravel, and other materials to filter water. You can do the same thing on a smaller scale.

1 Mix some soil or mud in water to make it dirty. Or get some cloudy water from a puddle or pond.

2 Place a funnel, or the cutoff top of a plastic bottle, in a glass jar. Put

a cone-shaped coffee filter in the funnel.

3 Dampen some clean sand and put a layer of this in the funnel.

4 Pour the dirty water slowly into the funnel. The sand traps larger particles, and the filter paper traps smaller ones.

5 The water that drips into the glass jar should look cleaner.

Warning: Do not drink this water—it may still contain harmful germs.

What happens when you turn on a faucet?

As you turn on a water faucet, you open a gap that allows the water in the pipe to come out. The water is always trying to push its way out, but it is stopped by a rubber washer that blocks the pipe. When you turn on the faucet, a screw lifts away from the washer. The water can then push the washer up and flow past.

MAKE A WASHER

You can see how a faucet works by making your own washer from soft modeling clay.

1 Put a blob of clay onto the end of a pencil. Fasten a piece of plastic wrap over it with a rubber band.

2 Press the clay washer into the neck of a cutoff plastic bottle. Hold the bottle upside down and fill it with water.

3 Lift the washer to let water flow. Press it down to close the tap.

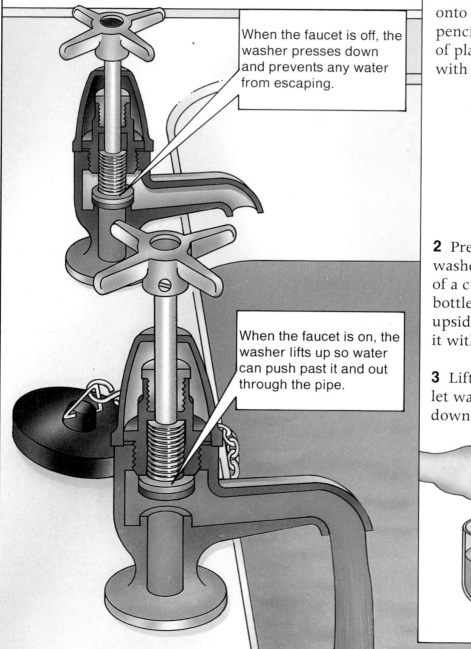

When the faucet is off, the washer presses down and prevents any water from escaping.

When the faucet is on, the washer lifts up so water can push past it and out through the pipe.

How do toilets flush?

Toilets flush by sending new water into the bowl. Inside the tank there is a compartment called a bell. When you press the handle, the water inside the bell goes into the bowl, sucking other water in the tank with it.

The handle works a lever that raises a disk in the bell. The disk lifts some water up, which pours into the bowl.

A float in the tank goes down as the water level falls. This makes a valve open so the tank can refill.

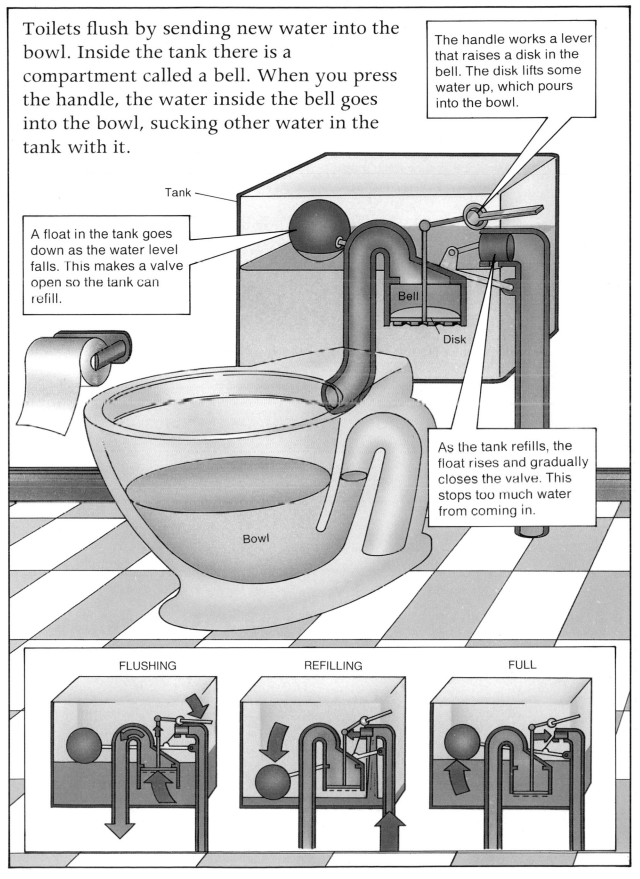

Tank

Bell

Disk

As the tank refills, the float rises and gradually closes the valve. This stops too much water from coming in.

Bowl

FLUSHING

REFILLING

FULL

What happens to all our garbage?

For many years, people have mixed up different types of garbage and thrown it all away, to be buried in enormous pits on land or put in containers sunk into the sea. However, we will gradually run out of places to dump garbage. We will also run out of the materials that are needed to make new things. Therefore, some garbage is now recycled — that is, remade so it can be used again.

DO YOU KNOW

Recycling saves on the fuel, like oil or gas, that is used to make things. Less heat is needed to recycle glass, paper, and tin than to make them from the beginning. So less fuel is used up to produce the heat.

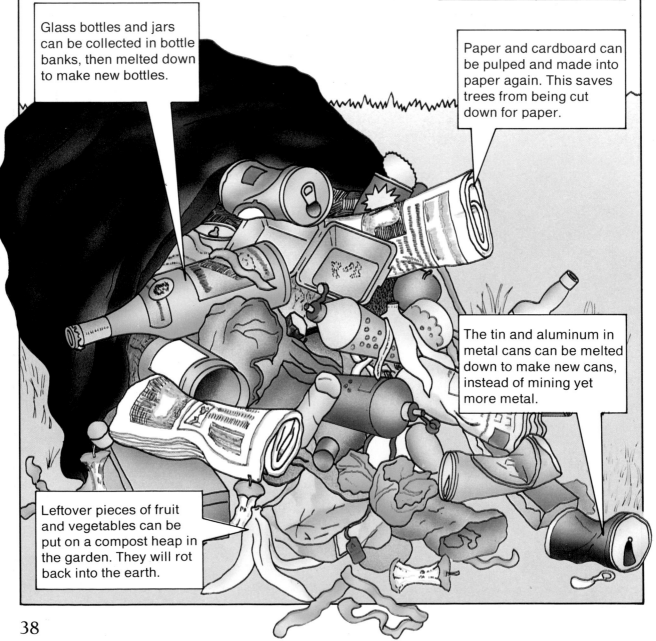

Glass bottles and jars can be collected in bottle banks, then melted down to make new bottles.

Paper and cardboard can be pulped and made into paper again. This saves trees from being cut down for paper.

The tin and aluminum in metal cans can be melted down to make new cans, instead of mining yet more metal.

Leftover pieces of fruit and vegetables can be put on a compost heap in the garden. They will rot back into the earth.

Useful words

Circuit   A circle around which an electric current flows.

Electron   An invisibly small particle, or piece of matter.

Evaporation   The process by which a liquid turns into a gas.

Insulator   A special material that prevents the passage of heat, sound, or electricity. For example, insulators help stop heat loss from ovens and vacuum bottles.

Microchip   A tiny electronic device containing many miniature circuits that can process or store electrical signals. Microchips are found in many machines, from calculators and computers to washing machines and cars.

Microphone   An instrument that picks up sound waves and turns them into electric waves that can pass along a wire.

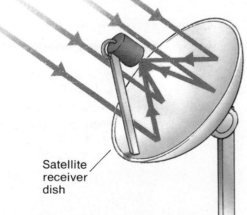

Satellite receiver dish

Microwave   A type of invisible wave similar to radio waves. Microwaves are often used to carry signals to satellites. Inside a microwave oven microwaves are beamed through food in order to cook it.

Recycle   To pass something through a series of treatments which allows it to be reused.

Reservoir   A lake that has been built to collect and store water.

Satellite   An object that circles another object. For example, the moon is a satellite of the earth. Artificial satellites are used for telecommunications.

Telecommunications   The sending and receiving of information by telephone, telegraph, radio, and television.

Thermostat   A device that controls temperature automatically. It switches off when too hot and on when too cold

Transformer   An instrument that increases or decreases the voltage, or strength, of an electric current.

Vacuum   A space that has nothing in it, not even air.

Valve   A device that controls the flow of a gas or liquid, usually allowing it to go in one direction only.

Index